Moses
God's Helper

WILLIAM E. YOUNG • ILLUSTRATED BY J. WILLIAM MYERS

BROADMAN PRESS
Nashville, Tennessee

© Copyright 1976 ● Broadman Press
All rights reserved
4242-25
ISBN: 0-8054-4225-1

Dewey Decimal Classification: J 221.92
Subject heading: MOSES
Printed in the United States of America

Contents

A Slave Becomes a Prince

Moses' father, Amram, and mother, Jochebed, had prayed for a child. When Moses was born in Goshen, a new Pharaoh had become ruler of Egypt.

Pharaoh called to his officers. "Deal harshly with the foreigners," he ordered. "There are too many of them. They are too strong."

This wicked Pharaoh was afraid of the Hebrews. He made them live as slaves. They were made to build cities, temples, palaces, and tombs for the Egyptians. They had to make their own bricks of straw, clay, and pitch (something like tar).

But the Hebrews did not become weak. They became strong. They had many more children.

Pharaoh ordered that all boy babies born to the Israelites be killed. There was great sorrow among the people. But they trusted God.

When Moses was born, his family hid him three months.

Jochebed made a basket-boat for Moses. She lined the boat with pitch and placed soft clothes in it. She and Miriam, Moses' sister, placed the boat containing Moses in the tall grass at the edge of the river Nile.

The princess, daughter of Pharaoh, and her friends discovered the basket. They took it from the water.

"This must be one of the Hebrews. The mother is trying to save her child. I will make the baby to be my own son," she said.

Miriam rushed to the princess and asked, "Would you like for me to find a nurse to care for the baby?"

The princess agreed for Miriam to find a nurse. Miriam ran for her mother.

"Take the baby home with you," the princess said to Jochebed. "Take care of him. I will pay you well. When he is old enough, bring him to the palace."

"I will call him Moses," the princess said.

Moses is an Egyptian name which means "taken out," because the princess had taken him out of the water.

When Moses was a strong boy, Jochebed took him to the palace. He lived as a prince at the palace for many years. But Moses still remembered that he was a Hebrew.

Moses grew into a strong, alert, well-educated young man. He was taught the wisdom of the Egyptians. Egypt had a great civilization. Moses learned about the things the wisest Egyptians knew about writing, building, and science.

In all his learning of how to be a prince, Moses never forgot that he was really one of the Hebrew slave people. He was sorry for his people, who worked under the wicked guards. Moses chose to worship God. He did not accept the Egyptian worship of the sun and the Nile River.

One day he saw an Egyptian beating a Hebrew. This made Moses angry. He looked around. He could see no one looking. He killed the Egyptian and hid his body in the sand.

The next day Moses met two Hebrew men who were fighting. Stepping between them, Moses scolded the man who was wrong. Moses asked him why he hit the other man. This made the man who had done wrong angry.

"You can't tell me what to do," he shouted. "Are you going to kill me like you killed that Egyptian?"

Moses was frightened. He knew it would not be safe for him to stay in Egypt.

Pharaoh heard what Moses had done. But before the guards could arrest Moses, he left Egypt.

Thinkback: On a separate sheet of paper, write at least five facts you learned about Moses.

A Runaway Prepares to Lead

Moses went to a country called Midian.

One day he sat down beside a well to rest and think. Seven sisters, daughters of Jethro, the priest of Midian, came to the well to water their father's sheep.

The girls filled the troughs with water. But some shepherds arrived, pushed the girls aside, and watered their own flocks at the full troughs. Moses jumped up and helped the girls to water the herd. When the girls got home, their father asked why they had come back so quickly.

"An Egyptian drove off the shepherds and helped us water the sheep," they told him.

"Where is the man?" their father asked. "Call him so that he can eat supper with us."

So Moses went home with them. He became a shepherd, working with Jethro. Moses married Zipporah, one of Jethro's daughters.

Moses walked with his sheep in this wilderness near Mount Horeb. He wore a coarse coat of a shepherd and carried a shepherd's staff. Day after day for forty years Moses had cared for his father-in-law's sheep. The sun and wind had tanned his face and hands. The years had whitened his hair. Moses looked very different from the young man who had lived in Pharaoh's palace.

"Why did I come to this wild and lonely country? Why am I a shepherd in this scrubby, desert land?" Moses asked himself. "What does the future have in store for me?"

Suddenly, Moses saw ahead of him a flaming fire. He ran closer to see what was happening. He saw that a bush was afire but was not burning up!

"Moses, come no closer. Take off your shoes. Walk in your bare feet, for the place you stand on is holy ground.

Moses knew at once that God was speaking to him. He covered his face with his hands so that he could not see the flames.

"I am the God of your father, the God of Abraham and Isaac and Jacob. I have heard the cry of my people in Egypt, and the time has come for them to leave Egypt."

"Come, I will send you to Pharaoh. You will bring my people of Israel out of Egypt to a land I will show you."

"But who am I?" Moses asked. "This job is too big for me to do."

Moses did not want to go back to Egypt. He was afraid. He offered excuses as to why he should not do what God asked him to do. God answered each excuse. God gave Moses wonderful powers so that the Hebrews would believe him.

"I will be with you and help you," said God. "Listen to my voice and obey it. Go back to Egypt, and prepare my people."

Moses knew God was speaking to him. He felt the presence of God.

Thinkback: Look at the map. Find the place where Moses went to escape death. Read Exodus 3:1-2. How did Moses know God was present?

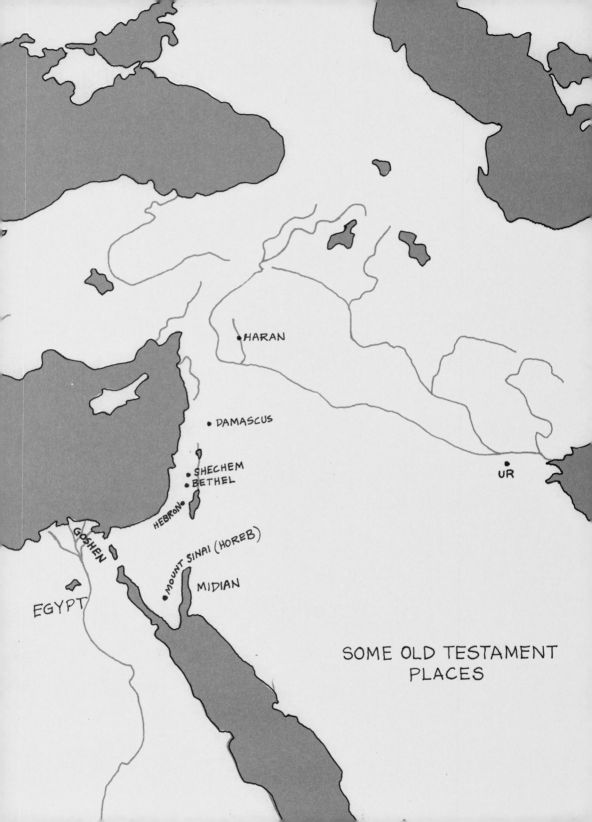

HARAN

DAMASCUS

SHECHEM
BETHEL
HEBRON

GOSHEN

MOUNT SINAI (HOREB)

MIDIAN

EGYPT

UR

SOME OLD TESTAMENT
PLACES

A Man of God Challenges a King

Moses obeyed God. He took his wife and sons and started for Egypt. On the way he met Aaron, his brother. Together, they returned to Egypt. They called the people together. Moses said. "God has sent me to lead you out of Egypt to another land where you will be free."

The people believed that God had sent Moses and Aaron to lead them out of Egypt.

Moses prayed to God. He went to Pharaoh. He spoke firmly, "The Lord, the God of the people of Israel, says to you, 'Let my people go.'"

"Who is the Lord of the people of Israel?" Pharaoh demanded. "I do not know this God. Why should I obey him? His people work for me. I will not let them go! They must work harder."

Nothing that Moses and Aaron could do softened the heart of Pharaoh. He feared the Hebrews, but he also wanted to keep them as slaves.

Moses asked again and again. Pharaoh said no again and again. He made the Hebrews work harder and harder.

Moses told Pharaoh terrible things would happen to Egypt and to Pharaoh's people. "The Lord, the God of the people of Israel, says, 'Let my people go,' " he said again.

One by one, terrible things happened to Egypt. The water and all streams of Egypt became blood. Seven days later frogs covered the land. Then followed plagues of gnats and flies. The cattle became sick. Later followed the plagues of boils, hailstorms, locusts, and darkness.

To stop each plague, Pharaoh agreed to let the Hebrews leave Egypt. But each time, he changed his mind and God sent another plague.

Pharaoh sent for Moses. "Get out of my sight!"

Bravely Moses answered, "God will send one more terrible plague upon you and your people. Then the Hebrews will leave your land."

That night God warned Moses and Aaron to tell all their people that each Hebrew family should kill a lamb. They were to sprinkle the lamb's blood on the doorposts of their house. Every house showing this sign was "passed over" and saved from destruction. This deliverance is remembered by the Jews until today as the Passover meal.

At last came the terrible night when all the firstborn children in Egyptian homes died. A great cry of sorrow rose from Pharaoh and his people.

The people of Egypt became afraid. Pharaoh's officers came to him. "Egypt is being ruined. Do what Moses says. Let the people of Israel go and worship their God. They are his people."

Pharaoh was afraid, too. He called Moses in the middle of the night. "Go away from Egypt," he said. "Go quickly. Take your flocks and herds with you."

"Get ready! Get ready!" These exciting words spread from house to house throughout the Israelite community of Egypt.

God's power had convinced Pharaoh at last that he was to set Moses and the Israelites free.

The people took all their flocks, herds, and cattle. They left in a hurry.

The journey out of Egypt started in darkness. Again, God showed his love for the Hebrews. He placed a pillar of fire ahead of them to light their way. When morning came, God changed the pillar of fire into a pillar of a cloud. The cloud by day and the fire by night became signs to the people of God's presence. These signs stayed with them until they reached the Promised Land.

Three days after the people began their journey, Pharaoh changed his mind. "The Egyptians are coming! The Egyptians are coming!" Panic swept among the people. The Hebrews knew they were no match for Pharaoh's soldiers. They hurried forward fearfully.

"Don't be afraid," Moses urged. "Trust God and move forward."

Moses raised his rod over the Red Sea and the waters parted. The Hebrews passed through safely. When Pharaoh's army followed, the drowning waters rushed together over them.

God's people were safe. Moses, Miriam, Aaron, and the Hebrews sang a song of praise and thanksgiving.

Thinkback: How did God care for the Hebrews as they left Egypt?

A Great People Cry for Food and Water

Safely across the Red Sea, the Hebrews were on their journey to Canaan.

Moses led the people to the south, away from the main road by the seacoast. They might meet enemy soldiers there.

For three days, the Hebrews marched without finding water.

At Marah they found water, but it was not fit to drink. God showed Moses how to make the water fit to drink by putting a certain tree into it. Soon the people were on the march again. After many days they came to Elim. There they found many shade trees and enough fresh water for everyone.

Then Moses led the people to move again. They traveled into the wilderness between Elim and Sinai. They ran out of food. The people forgot how God had helped them before. They blamed Moses. "We would rather have died in Egypt," they cried. "At least there we had bread to eat!"

God heard the people. "I will rain down food from heaven," he said to Moses.

Moses and Aaron told the people about God's promise. "You murmur and complain against God," Moses said. "What are Aaron and I? It is God who hears your grumbling. It will be God who gives you food."

That very evening many quail flew into the camp of the Hebrews. The people killed them to get fresh meat.

The next morning, when the dew had disappeared, the ground was covered with small, white, flake-like stuff. The people called it manna. They gathered it and made flat, honey-sweet cakes of bread from it. God had heard their cries and provided food.

The people journeyed to Rephidim. They complained to Moses because they had no water.

"What am I to do?" Moses prayed. "These people are about to kill me."

God was patient. "Lead the people to the foot of Mount Horeb," he spoke to his servant. "Go ahead of them. Take some elders with you. I will meet you there. Take your rod and strike the rock. Water will come out of the rock."

Moses obeyed God; and clear, cool water gushed out of the rock. There was enough to satisfy the thirst of every person in the camp.

Jethro, Moses' father-in-law, had learned of the Hebrews' journey. He came to visit Moses.

Moses told Jethro about God's blessings. Jethro was happy. He gave thanks for all that God had done for Moses and the Hebrews.

Moses had proved that he was a strong and wise leader. He was honest, fair, and trustworthy. The people knew he asked God's help with their questions. So they brought him all their problems.

"Moses, why are you trying to judge all these people yourself?" Jethro asked. "There is a better way. You must have help. Appoint good men as judges to help you. You will not have to listen to every argument. The special judges can listen and judge small complaints. As chief judge, you should hear only the important matters and bring these before God."

Moses followed Jethro's suggestions. He chose helpers. They were men who obeyed God.

Thinkback: How did God feed the hungry people?

A Man and a Mountain

The people traveled through the valleys and mountain passes. Finally they arrived at the foot of Mount Sinai, or Horeb. Here Moses had seen the burning bush nearly a year before. Here God sent Moses out to lead his people. Now he had brought the Hebrews here to Mount Sinai.

Moses and the Hebrews arrived at Mount Sinai three months after escaping Egypt. They stayed for over a year.

The great mountain was wrapped in a thick cloud. The lightning flashed. The long roll of thunder echoed around the top.

"I am coming to you in a thick cloud," said the voice of God to Moses, "that the people may hear when I speak. Obey my voice, keep my covenant, and you shall be a holy nation."

Moses knew that God loved these people. God wanted to make them into a great nation. He had promised Abraham long ago that he would use his descendants to bless the whole world. But first, they would have to choose to obey him, to depend on him, and trust him to provide for them. They had to learn his way before God could use them.

Moses climbed to the mountaintop and entered into God's presence. God made known his way for his people. Moses listened, and he talked with God.

Then Moses returned to the people. He told them God's law for his people. The people listened to Moses. They heard God's laws:

- Thou shalt have no other gods before me.
- Thou shalt not make unto thee a graven image.
- Thou shalt not take the name of the Lord thy God in vain.
- Remember the sabbath day, to keep it holy.
- Honor thy father and thy mother.
- Thou shalt not kill.
- Thou shalt not commit adultery.
- Thou shalt not steal.
- Thou shalt not bear false witness against thy neighbor.
- Thou shalt not covet.

The agreement between God and the people was made. God's will was their law. But how were they to keep God's commandments?

Moses decided to climb the mountain once more to engrave the Ten Commandments in stone. Aaron was to be in charge of the camp while Moses was on the mountain.

Moses vanished again into the cloud which still hung over the mountain. He was away from the people for forty days and nights.

The people became restless. They went to Aaron and said, "We think something has happened to Moses. Make us some gods to lead us."

Aaron agreed to what they wanted. "Bring me all your golden earrings," he told the people. He melted the gold. Then he formed it into a golden calf.

God told Moses what had happened. "They have forgotten my laws. I will punish them with a terrible punishment." Moses saw how angry God was. He prayed, "God, you promised our forefathers to make us a great nation. Spare the people."

God did not destroy the Hebrews. Moses
went down the mountain and found the
people worshiping the golden calf. In his
anger and disappointment, Moses broke the
stone tablets of the law which he had brought
with him. He destroyed the idol and told the
people, "You have sinned a great sin. I will
pray that God will forgive you."

Again, God heard Moses' prayer and
forgave the people.

Moses returned to the mountain to be with God. God gave Moses the Ten Commandments again. They were written on two tablets of stone.

Moses came down from the mountain and called the people together. He held up the stones on which the laws of God were written. He said, "These are the words which the Lord has commanded, that you should do them."

"All that the Lord has spoken unto us, that we will do," the people said.

"God wants to live among us," Moses said. "He wants us to build him a special place of worship. It will be a place where God can dwell and where we can come together to worship him."

God told Moses and the people how to make a tent, called a tabernacle. The people also were to make an ark, or chest, and to put the ark in the center of the tent.

The people brought gold, silver, and jewels. They made fine linen and beautiful cloth. They dyed rams' skins. Some brought the wood needed for the tent poles and furnishings.

Moses was pleased with the generous people. He told them, "God is pleased that you want to give."

Soon the tabernacle was finished. In the center of the tent stood the ark, overlaid with gold. And Moses put into the ark the tablets of stone on which were written the laws of God.

The cloud of God's presence covered the tabernacle. So long as the cloud stood still over the tabernacle, the people stayed where they were. When the cloud moved, the people packed and moved their tents where the cloud led. The cloud and this simple, movable temple were signs of the presence of God and the beginning of Israel's "temple worship."

Moses appointed Aaron and his sons as priests. They were to care for this tent of meeting and the worship of the people.

Thinkback: Name two important things that happened at Mount Sinai.

A New Nation with Old Problems

The Hebrews had now become a nation. Carrying the tent of meeting and the scrolls of the law, the people left Sinai. They moved on toward the borders of the Promised Land.

The people still grumbled about the lack of water and food. They experienced plagues and fought with desert tribesmen.

The cloud and people stopped next at Hazeroth. Here Miriam and Aaron showed they were jealous of their brother. "Why should Moses be chief ruler when God has sometimes spoken to us, too?" they wondered.

God showed Miriam and Aaron they were wrong. They apologized to Moses. Moses prayed to God to forgive them.

The cloud's next stop was the wilderness of Paran, just outside the land of Canaan.

Moses needed a plan to give the people courage to move forward. "Send twelve men to Canaan," God told Moses. One man from each tribe — twelve in all — was to gather information about the land and its people.

The spies traveled in the land of Canaan for forty days.

"It is a good land," they reported on their return. "But we cannot take it," ten of the spies reported. "We should enter the land and trust God to help us take it," said Caleb and Joshua. "Think of all God has done for us already. If we obey him, God will give us this land as he promised."

But the people were frightened. Their faith in God was weak.

God was disgusted with the people. Moses asked him to forgive the Hebrews. God forgave them but not without punishment. They were to stay in the wilderness until all the people who were twenty years or older on leaving Egypt had died — with the exception of Caleb and Joshua.

The Hebrews wandered in the wilderness in Zin and made camp at Kadesh. Here Miriam died and was buried.

About this time the wells at Kadesh dried up. The people complained. God told Moses, "Take Aaron and the rod and have all the people gather around the rock. Speak to the rock and water will flow out. There will be water for all the people and their cattle."

Moses and Aaron did as God told them. But they did not speak to the rock as God had commanded. Moses spoke to the people in an angry voice and asked, "Must we bring you water out of this rock?" He did not speak to the rock at all but hit it with his rod.

Water gushed out of the rock. There was enough for the people and their cattle to drink.

God was displeased. Moses and Aaron had disobeyed him. Moses had become angry and spoke unkindly to the people. He gave himself and Aaron credit for the miracle instead of God. And he struck the rock when God told him to speak to it.

God told Moses and Aaron, "Because you disobeyed, and the people thought you gave them the water instead of me, I will not allow either of you to lead these people into the land of Canaan."

For thirty-eight years the people wandered in the great wilderness. Then Moses planned to lead them to the border of Canaan near Edom. The king of the Edomite people refused to let the Hebrews go through Edom. So the people journeyed south and then east around Edomite territory.

At Mount Hor, Aaron died and was buried.

The people continued to grumble at Moses. They often turned away from the worship of the one true God. Each time, Moses brought them back to the God who was leading them. He gave them careful instructions in ways of worship. He also gave exact duties for their daily conduct.

Thinkback: Why did God punish Moses?

An Old Man Sees the Promise

Moses was growing old. The long years of desert life had made him tired. He knew he was about to die. He wanted to be sure the people would have another leader.

God told Moses, "Take Joshua. Lay your hands on him. Give him some of your honor so that all the children of Israel will obey him."

Moses obeyed God. He told the people, "I am one hundred and twenty years old. I am not able to lead you any longer. Remember that Joshua will lead you into Canaan."

"Be strong. Go with good courage. Do not be afraid. The Lord your God goes with you. He will not fail you or forsake you."

Moses climbed Mount Nebo and looked out into the land of Canaan. He knew his people would soon be in the land God had promised them.

Here Moses died. The people of Israel mourned for him for thirty days. They said, "Moses knew God and spoke with him as a friend." They sang a song of thanksgiving to God for Moses, who had led them to the Promised Land.

Moses was one of the greatest men who ever lived. He was the only person who ever talked with God face-to-face.

Thinkback: What special honor did God grant Moses before he died?

Reflections

Imagine . . .
- You are Moses.
- The desert is hot and you see nothing but sand for miles.
- You are wondering why God is leading you this way.

How do you *feel* about being free from slavery in Egypt? What do you *think* of the people? What do you *know* about God? How do you *feel* about God's care for you and the people in the wilderness? How do you *feel* about not being able to enter the Promised Land?

Think . . .
- Did Moses have a reason to thank God for his life? Why? Do you thank God for life? How do you show it?
- How did God use Moses to help his people? How can you help God?
- God was interested in Moses and his problems. How does God show you he is interested in you?